Healing Your Heart:

A 7-Day Devotional

Courtney Tate

ISBN: Paperback [979-8-9853708-2-9]

Published in Lancaster, SC
Second printing edition 2022.
Printed in the USA

CourtneySTate.com

Peace on the Other Side

Day 1

Isaiah 41:10 Don't be afraid, for I am with you. Don't be discouraged, for I am your God. I will strengthen you and help you.

Have you ever been faced with some big choices and you didn't want to make a decision for fear of how things might turn out? There was a time in my life that I was a little afraid of what starting my dating life over again might look like. However, I wasn't so afraid that I stuck around to see. Many times I have seen people stay in a relationship for fear of being alone. While I knew that wasn't my story, I absolutely dreaded the thought of starting over. After I finally took the leap and ended a long term relationship, the following year was quite the adventure. Instead of spending time worrying about what was or wasn't working, when to travel to spend time with my boyfriend, or other things to sustain a long distance relationship; I was able to: focus on work, grow my business, and enjoy some downtime. As a result, I got a promotion, was invited to an exclusive training to help advance my business, and every Sunday it seemed like God had the sermons lined up just for me. Trusting God to get to the other side allowed me to walk into my healing. It allowed me to forgive and find my peace with everything. God taught me that His peace was all I needed and that it would push me into my next season of life. As I reflect, I'm simply amazed at how God helped me come out healed, confident, and at peace on the other side.

Reflection Questions: What are you anticipating on the other side of your big decision? What would help you decide to take the first step to get to the other side? Can you imagine a life filled with peace not chaos...what does that look, feel, and sound like for you?

Talk to God as you answer those questions and ask Him to help you see yourself on the other side and experience His divine peace.

Change of Plans

Day 2

Proverbs 16:9 We can make our plans, but the LORD determines our steps.

I will never forget maybe 4-5 months post breakup thinking I had gotten over the hurdle. Then **BOOM** one day it hit me right in the face! For the past few years we discussed life and how it would change when we got married, had kids, and started our new life together. It was getting closer to the end of the year and I couldn't help but think about how I'd be starting 2020. Little did I know I would not be engaged, a bride or planning to become a mom as I had mapped things out before. I literally sat on the floor and cried telling Jesus how it wasn't fair that those things were no longer my current option. After a moment, I paused and cleaned up my face, I said out loud "Court, God didn't bring you here to leave you". In that moment and through my tears, I recognized that I needed to accept the seemingly sudden change of plans! Although it was perfectly okay to have had those conversations and plans it was time to accept that those things were no longer my immediate destiny. Alternatively, I was right where I needed to be at this point in my life and I really needed to embrace it. So, I did just that, I started talking to God and Proverbs 16:9 came to mind, I was in need of His direction. At that point I asked God to direct my path so that I'm less focused on checking off those items and more focused on what He wants from me in life. Being open to a change of plans allowed me to develop in other areas and focus on being ready as God directs my new journey.

Reflection Questions: What was a moment that you realized your plans had changed? How did you cope with that? Have you asked God to direct you on this new journey?

Talk to God as you answer those questions and ask Him to rewrite your story. Ask Him to take control and help you navigate your revised pathway.

Forgiveness is for You

Day 3

Ephesians 4:31-32 Get rid of all bitterness, rage and anger, brawling and slander, along with every form of malice. Be kind and compassionate to one another, forgiving each other, just as in Christ God forgave you.

In life and relationships we are all bound to be disappointed, heartbroken, or mistreated. In those moments as we process what happened to us, we are eventually faced with the option to forgive or not. I can think back to a time that someone very special to me caused hurt that cut deeper than I ever would have expected. I was sad and they appeared to lack any remorse over what had occurred. I would think about the situation and wonder why I wasn't fuming or irate, after all, they had mistreated me and I'd be justified to feel that way, right?! Sometimes friends, partners, or others that we love can cause pain and never realize the extent of the damage. Knowing that, I still wasn't mad or upset, I was just *really* hurt; even still I wanted the best for them. Every time I said that, friends gave me a funny look, then they would say "Court it's okay to be mad!". Again, I would explain I was genuinely okay and I actually prayed they wouldn't repeat the same thing with others. I remember being so hurt, that I sat in church and asked God to heal whatever they needed to help them not break the trust or inflict a similar type of pain on anyone else. Knowing I would never wish this hurt on others, I needed to heal enough to ensure I would not inflict this pain on a friend, future partner or others. The only way to do that was to let it go and forgive. I felt like my response was abnormal; I thought I should have been angry but God reminded me that He was walking with me every step of the way so walking in forgiveness was right. I couldn't harbor negative feelings, I had too much love for them and God. Therefore, God's love overshadowed the hurt. God's love made forgiveness come second nature. God's love made my healing process so much easier! Walking in forgiveness gave me so total peace, even in the most challenging moments.

Reflection Questions: Who or what has hurt you that you haven't yet forgiven? How can you leverage God's love to help you forgive? How can you leverage God's love to forgive yourself?

Talk to God as you answer those questions. Ask God to help you see that forgiveness is a gift to yourself. Ask God to help you forgive yourself. If you're still harboring unforgiving thoughts or feelings, allow God's love to help you to forgive that person.

Moving On

Day 4

Ecclesiastes 3:1-3; For everything there is a season, and a time for every matter under heaven: a time to be born, and a time to die; a time to plant, and a time to pluck up what is planted; a time to kill, and a time to heal; a time to break down, and a time to build up.

The decision to move on from a relationship and release any heartbreak or pain isn't always the easiest thing to do. After over 3 years I knew it was time to call it quits in my relationship. The hard part was still loving him and vice versa but it was obvious that we needed to part ways. Nothing prepared me for the 24+ hours of nonstop tears that followed. Although I was sad, I trusted God that it was best for me to move on. I prayed and checked in with God throughout the entire relationship, so that wasn't new for me. What was new was God showing me it was time to move on. I had so many questions: What do you mean? Do I really need to end things? I'm almost 34 years old so it's not possible you want me to start over...again?!

After asking those questions, I could not shake the feeling, so I knew it was time to let that relationship go. Saturday was a LONG day with many many tears but necessary. Moving on was hard, but I finally relented that if it was time to end this relationship I had to trust God and do the work. In choosing to trust God, the tears eventually stopped flowing. God led me to sermons, devotionals, and prayers reminding me of His promises. In those moments, I learned that moving on is not always easy but the peace that comes with the obedience makes it worth it every time.

Reflection Questions: What is in your life that God is pushing you to move on from? What's making you hold on to it still? What will it take for you to let it go and trust in God's plan?

Talk to God as you answer those questions and ask Him to help you move on to embrace what He has next for you.

The Power of Your Pause

Day 5

Psalm 62:5 Let all that I am wait quietly before God, for my hope is in him.

If you told me in the midst of things that God would pull me through, I never would have believed it would happen the way it did. Coming out of a breakup that I thought would end in marriage was scary and heartbreaking, but also a relief. However, through a mix of emotions, God helped me to get to the other side. He helped me to see in my most vulnerable moments that He was with me and would guide me through it. God showed me that if I leaned into Him and the Word that I could fully heal without all of the malice and negativity that so many people experience. Healing only started to happen when I was willing to pause. After engaging in many conversations with friends, listening to my latest playlist, and so many other distractions, it was time to pause. Pausing would mean protecting my quiet time, removing the outside noise, being still, and sitting with my emotions. This included sitting in my cubicle for THREE hours bawling. This was the catalyst that propelled me into my new normal.

My new normal meant fighting the urge to talk about it for hours, continuing to forgive myself and others, and making more time for God. It was most helpful when I had conversations with God; nothing formal, just sharing my heart whenever I felt the need, especially when I could get quiet to listen. Finding sermons to feed my spirit through the week, playing worship music, journaling, and focusing on feeling like myself again were all parts of the journey. I continued this process until one day I exhaled and was at peace. Meaning, I could talk to and about my ex without sad feelings brewing, think of the change in plans without getting emotional, and most importantly, I could think about what was next in life without worrying about my current status.

There is so much power in healing before you venture into your next relationship. The power in aligning yourself with God, knowing your worth, your value, and finding your voice prevents the potential for additional pain for you and/or your future partner. It's not worth it so remember the power of pausing to connect with God in those quiet moments. The power of pausing is reflected in my embrace and love of every part of this journey.

Reflection Questions: Have you taken time to pause and focus on God? Where are you on your journey? Do you have a scripture, song, or sermon that has resonated with you during your quiet time with God?

Talk to God as you answer those questions and ask Him to help you to pause, reflect and listen to Him while you're on this journey.

God Wants to Heal You

You

Day 6

Psalm 147:3 He heals the brokenhearted and bandages their wounds.
Jeremiah 30:17; For I will restore health to you, and your wounds I will heal, declares the Lord.

One Saturday, I spent the entire day crying and upset. These emotions caused me to hesitate to attend church on Sunday. I literally wanted to sit in bed and cry but I felt a push to be at church. Moment of honesty, I went with zero expectations but I did ask God to help me contain my emotions. When the pastor shared the new series on relationships I wanted to get up and walk out. Obviously, listening to someone talk about relationships was not of interest to me but I knew God wouldn't lead me astray so I listened, and took notes. Over the course of the next few weeks I was able to take nuggets away from the series but the craziest thing would happen when I prayed at home and church; I would literally find myself praying to God for my ex to heal. I could no longer hold on to the disappointment that I initially carried. While I selfishly didn't always like it, inside I knew that I could miss my healing if I didn't follow God's prompting to pray. In those moments, I am glad that I was obedient and surrendered to God's guidance. As time went on I still had good and bad days as I faced my new reality but I continued to talk to God and allowed Him to heal me. He spoke to me through the books I read, my prayer time, sermons and journaling. I learned about my missteps and oversights, to give myself grace, and even a man that I love isn't always the best option (timing is also important). Most importantly, I learned that God wasn't keeping score on any of the things that I just listed! He actually wanted to show me that He still has greatness in store for me! The beginning of the healing process was an adjustment but each and every day God was right there with a sermon, listening ear, person to chat, or just comfort in knowing that He was with me. God wanted to heal me.

Reflection Questions: When was your moment of knowing that God had healed you? What are those places in your life or your heart that still need to be healed by God? How can you let God heal you?

Talk to God as you answer those questions and ask Him to heal you. The journey isn't necessarily an easy one but embrace it! Take note as He speaks to you.

Preparing for Your Future Mate

Day 7

Phillipians 4:6 Don't worry about anything; instead pray about everything. Tell God what you need, and thank Him for all he has done.

After a significant amount of time focusing on my healing, I soon began to talk to God about being ready for my future spouse. As I prayed for him, sometimes I would start bawling at the thought of the unknown. Every time, God would comfort me with a reminder that there were still options for me. While reading about the tiny details to pray for in my future husband, I was in awe of how much God truly cares about this area of our lives! In those moments I paused to ask for forgiveness for my complaints and thanked God for the promises and desires of His heart for me!

As much as I pray that my spouse is ready for me, it is crucial that I am ready for my spouse. I know that it is equally important to pray for God to prepare me to be a great spouse. On a regular basis, I pray that God will: teach me to love unconditionally, guide and protect my heart, show me personal areas of growth, and bring people into my life that can serve as mentors.

Whether you recently ended a relationship, have wounds from the past or a broken heart, know that God cares about restoring and mending your heart. Trust God to build you to readily receive love again! Allowing God to heal your heart starts the journey to equip you to develop a lasting love and discover who you are and how you show up in a relationship. Always keep in mind how much God desires to be an active part in your healing journey and to continuously prepare you for your future mate!

Reflection Questions: Have you started to pray to God about your future spouse? Do you know what you desire in a partner? When you pray do you ask God to prepare you to be a spouse? What are some things that you can start to work on to prepare to be your best self in relationships?

Talk to God, ask Him to help prepare you for your future mate. Tell God what you are believing in Him for and add your spouse to your prayer list!

Closing Prayer

The past seven days together have been amazing as we were open and honest with God about where we are and our desire for His healing in our hearts. Prayer throughout this process was paramount in leading me from pain to healing! I have smiled as I shared this journey and how far along I've come with you. Hopefully you have taken time to write and reflect as you spent time unpacking your emotional bags to ultimately step into your own personal healing. I pray that this devotional has blessed you as much as it's been a blessing to share my journey with you! As we spend our final moments in prayer, share your heart with God and allow Him to come in and join you. During this prayer, open your heart and speak your truth in this time alone with God.

~CT

Heavenly Father,

Thank You for this time to connect and share our hearts with You, we are grateful for the chance to pause and listen for Your wisdom and guidance. God we ask that You forgive us now for any unrepented sin in our lives, so that You can be glorified. Right now, we come knowing that You have heard our thoughts, questions, and words that are spoken and unspoken. We ask that You take the areas of hurt and heal us. We call forth Your anointing to supernaturally heal the brokenhearted and downtrodden that are seeking You in this moment. Lord, we ask You to speak to us, You said where two or three are gathered You are in our midst. So, we thank You for Your presence right now, for mending our hearts and releasing vision and favor to each of us. We ask that You would speak to us individually to give us guidance and faith to trust You with our next. We cancel any and every attack and assignment that the enemy will try to bring against us and speak life into our situations in the name of Jesus. Lord, have Your way in our lives; lead and guide us in each decision that we make. Help us to hear You in our everyday lives. Guide us to be the mate You have called us to be. We pray that wives and husbands will walk in alignment and no division will stand in their homes. We thank You for opening the flow of communication in homes and for the restoration that will come. Lord open our ears to hear from You and our hearts to be ready to receive love again. Lord, we thank You now, we give You all the glory, it's in the most precious name of Jesus we pray, Amen.

Acknowledgements

Seeing a simple note in my phone turn into a devotional still blows my mind! I never imagined God would use a moment in my life to help others to heal and reflect. I have the best family and friends in the world and I am truly grateful to have each of you in my life! Thank you to everyone that listened when I shared my story and allowed me to process. A special thanks to those that assisted with the final touches, it means more to me than you will ever know.

Thank you for your support! Follow my author journey at CourtneySTate.com.

IG: @CourtneyTateWrites

Courtney Tate

About the Author

Courtney Tate is a veteran educator with thirteen years of educational experience. She is originally from Gastonia, NC and has been a resident of Charlotte, NC for the past 13 years. As an educator, she has been devoted to providing children with a quality education, developing teacher leaders, and making a positive impact in her community. Courtney is a lover of reading and started a book club to bring like minded women together. Courtney has been a follower of Christ since her childhood and served in various capacities at the local church. She lives a Christ inspired life each day!